A Day at the Track

By
Kelly Noll

Photos by
Kelly Noll, Leon Fox & Lara Paparo

OWL PUBLISHING

Owl Publishing, LLC.

150 Parkview Heights Road

Ephrata, Pa 17522

717-925-7511

www.OwlPublishingHouse.com

Copyright © 2017 Kelly Noll

ISBN: 0997906537

ISBN 13: 978-0997906530 (Owl Publishing, LLC.)

Library of Congress Control Number: In Progress

Disclaimer: Motocross is an inherently dangerous sport, and much of the action depicted in this book is potentially dangerous. Virtually all of the riders seen in our photos are experienced in motocross, and are supervised by experienced individuals, parents, and race officials. Do not attempt to duplicate any stunts that are beyond your own capabilities. Always wear the appropriate safety gear.

We're at the **motocross track!** Come with us and see everything riders do on race day.

The day begins early in the morning. Sometimes riders even **camp** at the track with their families. Some people sleep in a tent, or in their trailer or in a motor home.

The first thing to do is sign up for races. Riders have to pick the right class* for their age and type of dirt bike.

*A class is the group of riders that race together. They are usually the same age and have the same sized bikes.

Kids as young as
four can race!

4

Boys and girls can race.

It's time to get dressed!

Motocrossers wear a lot of protective gear and **never** ride without a helmet.

Motocross Gear

Helmet

Goggles

Neck Brace

Chest Protector

Jersey

Gloves

Pants

Boots

Motocrossers ride **dirt bikes** when they are racing.

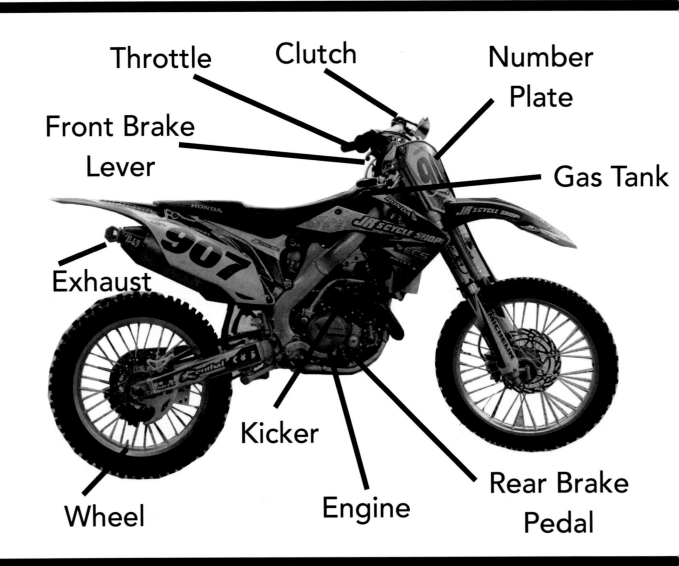

Throttle

Clutch

Number Plate

Front Brake Lever

Gas Tank

Exhaust

Kicker

Wheel

Engine

Rear Brake Pedal

What do these parts do?

Throttle: Make it go fast!

Clutch: Ready to shift gears?

Brakes: When we need to stop!

Kicker: Start the bike!

Now it's time for one last check on the dirt bikes before practice. Does everything work?

Is the gas turned on?   **Check!**

Is the tank filled?   **Check!**

Is there air in the tires?   **Check!**

Then practice starts. The riders look for the best line through the track. Ruts start to form in the mud.

Don't get stuck!

When practice is over, the National Anthem plays and everyone faces the American flag.

As the riders wait for the race to start they like to talk to each other. They share tips and figure out how to handle different parts of the track together.

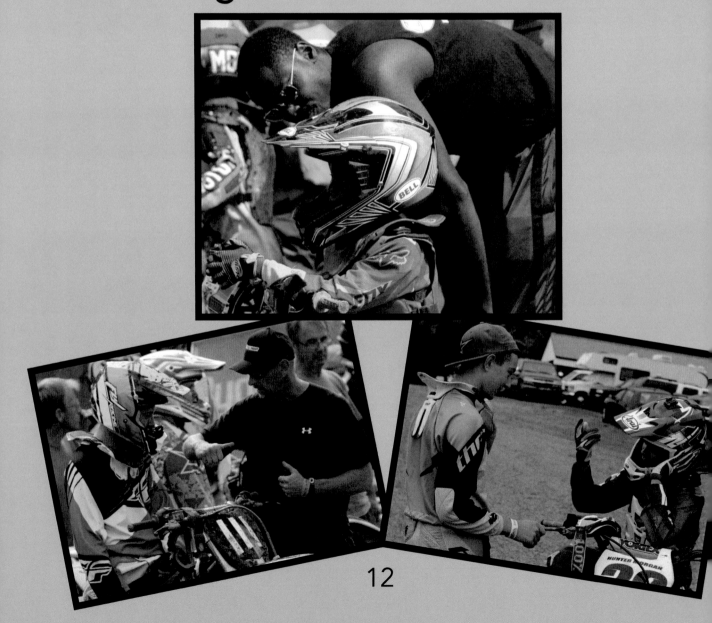

Motocrossers like to help each other.

Riders get their goggles on and fasten their helmets. It is important to always be safe.

The racers are anxious to get started! Friends help the riders push their bikes to the starting gates.

Moms and dads help pack down the dirt in front of the bikes for a smooth start.

The race is about to begin. The **roaring** engines echo across the track.

On the smaller bikes, moms and dads lift up the back of the bikes as the rider twists the throttle and **REVS** the bike, clearing out the engine.

Line up! Now it's time for the first race. Each class races two times. A race is called a **moto**. The riders can hardly wait!

19

The card holder points at the riders and they nod if they are ready.

They are all ready!

They watch for the gate to drop, **revving** their engines loudly.

21

The gate drops and the bikes take off at **top speed!** They all want to be first. The rider in the front at the first corner has the *holeshot*.

22

*A holeshot means the rider is in first place at the first corner of the race.

Around the track they **zoom**, each rider trying to get past the others.

One lap done!

The riders hit the jumps, **flying** high in the air and landing safely.

27

Now they go over a row of little jumps, called whoops*.

*Whoops are a series of little jumps in row.

Hurry!

Here comes the next rider!

Two laps done!
The leader has switched many times.

Who will win?

Oh No! **Crash!** The racers got too close to each other. They are tangled in a heap.

The riders may be banged or bruised, but they want to finish the race. Motocrossers are **tough** and want to do their best!

It's the **FINAL** lap!

Who will go past the checked flag
FIRST?

Winner!

It was an exciting race! The riders are happy that they tried their best, even if they didn't win. The riders congratulate each other.

It is time to get the **trophies!**

Race day is over.

Will you be at the next one?

See you there!

To Colby, who inspired this book.

This book also for all the young riders who demonstrate their drive, talent and courage each time they get on a dirt bike. Helmets off to you! Have fun and ride smart!

About the Author

Kelly Noll has a degree in Early Childhood Education and has been a teacher for over 20 years. She enjoys sharing her love of books with young children and finds it especially valuable to explore books on subjects that interest them.

Kelly lives in Pennsylvania with her husband, Corey, their son, Colby, their beloved pit bull, Rocky and their anti-social cat, Holeshot. Kelly has been a moto-mom and wife for 12 years and counting.

Thank you to Pagoda Motorcycle Club and Rocket Raceway and all the riders and parents. Thank you to my wonderful parents for all their support and love through the years. And to my husband and best friend, Corey, a thank you just isn't enough. You are my rock. I love you.

Made in the USA
Monee, IL
19 November 2020